Beneath the Lantern's Glow

Sketches and Stories from Southeast Asia and Japan

Words and illustrations by
Candace Rose Rardon

For Hannah, Jenny, and Kim,
and the inspiration you were in Goa.

Many thanks to Brooke Van Groningen for her design assistance, to Erin Ridley for her unbeatable editorial eye, and to Nina Johansson for permission to quote from the trailer for her book, *Drawing Around Sagrada Família.*

For more information or to contact Candace, please visit her website, *The Great Affair,* at www.candaceroserardon.com.

To order prints and greeting cards featuring sketches from this collection, please visit www.serendipitysketches.com.

Printed and bound in the United States

Table of Contents

Introduction

"Drawing the world really makes life a richer experience." – Nina Johansson

On my final night in Siem Reap, I walked its dusty streets alone, feeling outside myself.

Neon-lit bridges cast shimmering reflections on the canals below; backpackers and locals alike were beginning to filter into clubs; and on I walked, feeling like I was looking down at the country from above, like I could never understand what it went through, and is still going through.

I walked until I was lost, until I no longer knew from which direction I had come. And that's when I saw them: glowing red lanterns strung one after another down a dark and narrow alley. I followed the lanterns until the end, where I sat on a swinging bench and pulled out my sketchbook.

By this point in my journey, lanterns had become a kind of motif for me – from those in Kuala Lumpur's Chinatown to the large red lanterns sat outside Japanese temples – so much so that I had already decided on the title for this collection of sketches and sketch stories: *Beneath the Lantern's Glow*. And when I sat on the swing that night in Siem Reap and looked up, I knew instantly that I was looking at this book's cover.

There was a single round lantern directly above my head, floating over two banana trees and a yellow bicycle; each a fitting symbol of my six weeks in the region. On a night when I'd felt entirely disconnected from the city, I was suddenly right where I needed to be.

I was beneath the lantern's glow.

My vision for this book is three-fold: The following twenty sketches have been ordered chronologically, so that you might feel as if we are sitting down together, flipping through my actual sketchbook. Furthermore, I want it to seem as though you are journeying through this fascinating corner of the world yourself: smelling apple shisha in Singapore, sharing in the wonder of Angkor Wat, and walking the hills of Shodoshima, Japan, and Vang Vieng, Laos.

Lastly, I hope that the many serendipitous encounters that unfolded with each sketch will leave you open and inspired to seek connections in your own life; that every moment will hold magic and, when you least expect it, you too will find yourself beneath the lantern's glow.

Shophouses and shisha on Bussorah Street

Sketching Singapore

It's a Sunday night in Singapore and the air is sweet with the scent of apple shisha.

I'm only in town for the weekend, visiting my friends Bridget and Manisha, but already I know that it's here – in the heart of the Arab Street neighborhood – that I will look back on as my favorite corner of the city.

I find such enclaves of a culture fascinating, the way they instantly transport you from one world to another. One minute, you're in what feels like Asia's cleanest city; the next minute, simply by crossing the street, you're in the Middle East. Shisha pipes gurgle, the call to prayer sounds, shop signs are written in Arabic, and women pass by in black *hijabs*, their husbands in prayer caps and white tunics.

Gone are the sleek and shiny skyscrapers that form the city's skyline, lined up in smooth shades of glass and steel. In their place are two-story shophouses with clay tile roofs and shuttered windows, painted in bold tones of pink and purple and blue.

"This is how all of Singapore used to be," Manisha tells me, and I can't help wishing I'd seen it then.

But what strikes me the most on Bussorah Street – formerly known as Sultan Road, after the golden-domed Sultan Mosque at one end of it – are the smells. While walking back to Bridget and Manisha's flat on Saturday afternoon, I stopped in my tracks and took in a big breath. And then I took another, and another, each time growing more and more perplexed.

The thing was, I couldn't smell anything – and after living in a place like India, where the air is a constant mix of the sweetest and foulest scents in the world, it was an odd revelation.

But not so in this part of Singapore. From swirling shisha smoke to roasting lamb, the smells are back – and for that, I love Arab Street all the more.

The call to prayer sounds, rising above the chatter of diners.
Bussorah Street
ARAB STREET, SINGAPORE.
31.3.2013, 8pm.
The air swirls with the scents of apple shisha, roasting lamb, and Turkish coffee — divine. Our waiter Hassam Baba, who moved here three years ago from Istanbul, stares over my shoulder and says, "Same real."

I sit at a
red plastic table
at Tang Cha
snow ice shop,
sipping a ice honey
lime drink and
singing along to
the pop songs they
keep playing —
"We R who We R,"
"DJ Got Us Falling
in Love Again"...
Jalan Petaling
CHINATOWN, KUALA LUMPUR.
1 APRIL 2013 19.30
A thousand flavors
float in the air; my
stomach growls.
The street i
one never em
no face even
the same — it
seems like the
whole world i
in this city.
A rat scurri
through a
restaurant, Jim
says, "Micke

Chinese lanterns on Petaling Street

Sketching Malaysia

I arrive in Kuala Lumpur ready to walk as long as it takes to find a view to sketch.

My steps lead me first to the great green gate of Jalan Petaling – the well-known main road of Chinatown called Petaling Street. Where two men stand roasting chestnuts, sifting them through hot coals in a round silver vat, I turn left, ready to keep walking. But it's then that I see them: zig-zagging rows of red Chinese lanterns, strung above my head from one lamp post to another, glowing like hollow pumpkins.

They alternate in shape between spherical and oblong, in striking contrast to the neat square windows of the building behind them, and I'm suddenly reminded of the first time I saw such lanterns.

Ever since visiting Macau three years ago, these lanterns have never failed to fascinate me. I find them incredibly evocative – a symbol, perhaps, that I have truly arrived Elsewhere.

I wonder if such symbols exist for everyone, something that represents just how far we've traveled from home, no matter where home may be for each of us in the world.

Here in Kuala Lumpur, I have to sketch these lanterns, that much I know – but from where? Finally I spot a shop, a small ice cream stand with just two red plastic tables out front and two yellow umbrellas overhead.

Soon after I begin, a woman with a British accent but of Middle Eastern origin, *hijab* scarf covering her head, stands over my shoulder and studies the sketch I did in Singapore. I tell her about my plan to spend six weeks sketching around Asia.

"That's wonderful," she says. "You should do a book."

It's the kind of moment where the universe seems to affirm the very thing you've set out to do.

I smile, thank her, and say, "I am." Tonight, inspiration didn't take long to find.

In the center of it all in the Ginza district

Sketching Japan

On a sunny Tuesday afternoon in Tokyo, I emerge from the Ginza subway station on the hunt for a building I can't remember the name of.

After searching online and coming across a landmark called the Wakō Building, it seemed like an appropriate subject for a sketch. Built in 1932, it sits right in the heart of the Ginza shopping district – what you might call the Fifth Avenue of Tokyo, lined as it is with Prada, Cartier, Bvlgari, and a hundred other luxury shops – and yet at first the building is nowhere to be found.

I walk on, losing myself in the crowds, loving the vertical signs that hang from each storefront, until I notice the district section numbers (Ginza 4, Ginza 5) keep growing larger. I still have much to learn about Japan, but I take this to mean I'm getting farther away from the heart of Ginza, and thus from the Wakō Building.

Not two seconds after turning around, it suddenly appears, with its famous Seiko clock tower chiming in two o'clock and its many windows reflecting the sun. But not only that – right across the street is a two-story coffee shop called Le Café Doutor.

The café has beautifully curved, floor-to-ceiling windows that overlook the intersection and provide an ideal vantage point from which to view the Wakō. The only problem is that all of Tokyo seems to feel the same way.

But only ten minutes later, a seat opens up and I sweep in, claiming my spot with a pearl iced au lait. I spread out my sketching supplies, ready to begin, when I glance down at the intersection and am soon transfixed by the blur of pedestrians forming an endless stream over each crosswalk. I feel like I've come to the center, where the very pulse of this country originates.

On a Tuesday in Tokyo, I found the Wakō after all – and so much more.

Ginza Main Street
TOKYO, JAPAN
9 APRIL 2013 14.00
MITSUKOSHI GINZA
Two grey-haired Japanese men sit down next to me, both wearing caps and wind-breakers. One bears a tray of bagels and coffee.

Rain beats against the windows, men in suits and ties and neon orange jackets alike take shelter inside
fish tank
The men smoke, tip their ashes in canary yellow ashtrays.
sugar
magazines
toothpicks
violets in a glass ashtray
chili
As I sketch, I think of what Kawai said at lunch – "This is chopsticks country."
Still life in the Souvenir Shop
SHODOSHIMA ISLAND, JAPAN.
11 APRIL 2013 14.00
drip coffee

Still life in a Shodoshima souvenir shop

Sketching Japan

The rain starts not long after I arrive on Shodoshima.

I've come to this small island in Japan's Seto Inland Sea to walk a 100-mile pilgrimage called the 88-Temple Circuit. But before I begin, I've given myself a day to settle in. As it is, I'm okay with the rain – for today.

The one problem is that my plan to do a sketch of the island's rugged hills is now thwarted, and I find myself running for cover into a souvenir shop by the ferry terminal. The shop just happens to have a long counter with a few bar stools. I grab one, order a coffee, and look around for some back-up inspiration.

But then it occurs to me that sometimes the best thing to sketch is what's right in front of you. And what's in front of me here in a Shodoshima souvenir shop is a wonderfully eclectic mix of objects: a wooden container of disposable chopsticks, a fish tank, three violets growing in a glass ashtray, and an olive branch placed in a vase – a perfect still life if I ever saw one.

It's only while I'm laying the scene out in pencil that the sketch takes on a new layer of meaning: This time last year, I was walking the Camino de Santiago pilgrimage across Spain – and among the thirty pounds of mostly unnecessary stuff in my backpack was a book called *One Sketch a Day: A Visual Journal.*

There was a lot of rain on the Camino, too, so a large number of my sketches were done indoors.

"You draw many bars," one barista astutely observed, but only because there were so many along the way, where you could get a *café con leche* and wring the rain out of your clothes.

Before reaching Shodoshima, I'd wondered if there would be any connections between this pilgrimage and the Camino – beyond the obvious, of course. As I sip my Japanese drip coffee, yet again taking cover from the rain, it seems I've found my answer.

Temples and tiered roofs on a Japanese pilgrimage

Sketching Japan

Despite what its number might suggest, Temple 58 is only my second temple on the 88-Temple Circuit around Shodoshima Island.

Everything in me knows I should keep moving – after all, I have another six temples to see today alone and I've yet to leave the port town of Tonoshō.

But I find myself slipping off my backpack anyways, pulling out my sketchbook, and finding a seat in the bell tower just opposite the temple. As dark clouds curl across the sky, I wonder if I'll be able to capture the temple's vivid vermillion woodwork or the mystically twisted branches of the bonsai pine tree next to it.

Most of all, what I want to remember is the tiered roof. As with Chinese lanterns, I also have a thing for pagodas, ever since sketching those in Kathmandu's Durbar Square. While it means my first day on the circuit will be longer than it should, I can't help but sketch this temple.

Although I don't know it right now, here on the floor of the bell tower, Temple 58 is the only temple on the Shodoshima circuit with a layered roof. The rest I'll come across will vary tremendously in size and shape, but none will have such a roof.

What I also don't know in this moment is that eight days from now, when I finally reach the summit of Temple 56 – my last temple on the circuit – and begin my descent back into Tonoshō, the first thing I'll see as I look down at the city will be the roof of Temple 58 – right where I sketched it a week earlier.

Seeing it again will remind me of how different an experience this circular pilgrimage has been from the more linear Camino I walked last year – that by finishing where you began, your anticipation of reaching the end feels strangely akin to the anticipation of coming home.

It is the same but different – and, hopefully, so are you.

Temple No. 58
SHODOSHIMA 88-TEMPLE CIRCUIT
12 APRIL 2013 12 NOON
Granite pillars
surround the temple;
their kanji
indecipherable
to me.
When the wind blows,
which it does often, they stir
a few bells hanging from the roof
to life; their low melodic din
is a welcome sound.

Oranges and openness on Shodoshima Island

Sketching Japan

I have only begun to round a curve on the west coast of Shodoshima when he walks towards me – a workman whose name I learn is Sakamoto-san, a scarf tied several times around his neck, almost touching his gray, well-groomed beard.

As soon as he'd seen my pilgrim's white kimono jacket, he'd gone straight to the passenger seat of his little blue work van. Now he approaches, right arm extended with a single orange in his hand. I can't help wondering if he is giving me part of his lunch, or if he keeps a bag of them on hand for such occasions.

The orange is what is known as *o-settai*, Japanese for "welcome" or "reception," and is customarily given to pilgrims as an act of service; sometimes it's a small gift of food, other times a sweet-smelling sachet or pin. It isn't my first *o-settai* on the trail, but something about the spontaneity and simplicity of his gesture moves me the most.

Sakamoto-san drives away immediately after depositing the orange in my hands, but I linger on the road. Before me is a simple island garden: two tin-roofed wooden buildings, cherry trees still in bloom, and neat rows of onion patches – ubiquitous around Shodoshima. So elegant does this pastoral scene strike me that I sit right along the highway, just on the other side of the guardrail, to sketch it.

Later, after I resume walking, I pass the garden's driveway and see a sign out front – "Yasuke Park," it reads, "Wellcome!! Free."

What I'd taken to be someone's private backyard is actually open to the public. This incredible openness – for the smallest of gardens to welcome visitors, for a man to stop what he is doing to give a pilgrim an orange – has overwhelmed me again and again on this path.

I peel and sink my teeth into Sakamato-san's gift as I walk – an orange never tasted so sweet.

A veritable forest of cherry trees is miraculously still in bloom.
I sketch from the side of road no. 253.
An Island Back Garden
SHODOSHIMA, JAPAN
13 APRIL 2013 13.00

We have four seasons in an hour, from rain to warm sun to a wintry breeze.
Ryoanji Rock Garden
RYOANJI TEMPLE, KYOTO, JAPAN
21 APRIL 2013 12.30.

The universe in a moment at Ryōan-ji

Sketching Japan

On my first morning in Kyoto, I am sitting on the long wooden steps of the *hōjō*, the abbott's residence of Ryōan-ji Temple – one of 1,600 temples in this historic city.

At my feet is the temple's famous *kare-sansui,* or Japanese rock garden. In a small rectangle of white gravel, measuring just twenty-five by ten meters and raked to perfection by the monks each morning, sit fifteen stones. They've been arranged in such a way that they are never all visible from the same vantage point.

At first, I am tempted to move up and down the veranda, to try and spot every stone. And at the same time, there is much that moves with me: the weather, shifting from sunshine to wintry winds in a matter of minutes, as well as the crowds, also shifting in and out, debating in a dozen tongues whether or not they can spot the fifteenth stone.

But what never move are the stones themselves – and I realize that perhaps this is the test of Ryōan-ji, and its secret.

"Every moment has a little universe in it," says my friend Don, who has brought me here, and indeed I am struck by how the entire world can be felt in this moment, even when seated for hours in the same spot. Despite that elusive stone, there is still much to be felt and experienced: all the nationalities represented by other tourists, all the centuries of time embedded in the moss and gravel, all the students from across the country, who are delighted when I manage even one word of Japanese.

Inscribed on a nearby stone washbasin, which dates to the 17th century, is a four-character message that reads, "I learn only to be contented," or according to a different translation, "What one has is all one needs."

Here at Ryōan-ji, I can feel this to be true – that with or without the fifteenth stone, the moment is always, forever, enough.

Blessings on a bridge in Kōyasan

Sketching Japan

You hear them before you see them: the monks and pilgrims, walking through the Okunoin on a brisk Tuesday morning.

Home to over 200,000 gravestones, the Okunoin has been called the most sacred place in Kōyasan, itself one of the most sacred cities in the country. It was settled in 819 by Kobo Daishi, founder of the Shingon sect of Buddhism, and it is to his mausoleum that all paths through the cemetery lead – the very paths the monks and pilgrims walk.

As the monks grow near, it is the sound of their wooden sandals (known as *geta*) going clickety-clack against the cobblestones that precedes them. The pilgrims, however – dressed in their white kimonos and conical straw hats – are betrayed by the bells on their walking poles, which jingle each time the poles strike the path.

As for me, for once I'm not moving on a sacred path through Japan, having just completed the Shodoshima circuit. In Kōyasan, I instead find a spot on the Nakanohashi Bridge and let the path move around me as I sketch.

The pilgrims walk steadily along the cedar-lined way, but it's a group of thirty monks I'll remember the most. They never stop walking, but when they see what I'm up to, they crane their necks and wish me *ganbatte* a hundred times as they pass.

It's a phrase I learned well on the pilgrimage, loosely translated as, "Be strong, keep going, don't give up!" I loved saying *ganbatte* to other pilgrims on Shodoshima, and love the chance to do so in Kōyasan, too. To then hear it again in return – this time in regards to my sketching – feels almost like I'm being showered in blessings by these kind-hearted monks, their black robes swishing in time to their steps.

We may have come to the Okunoin for different reasons, but I have a feeling we'll each walk away just as blessed.

Nakanohashi Bridge
KOYA-SAN, JAPAN.
23 APRIL 2013 10.00.
t beneath
anopy of
-year-old
ar trees
Incense wafts
over from a small
shrine.
monks pass by,
their wooden sandals
going clickety-clack
on the stone.
you can hear the
pilgrims approaching
before they arrive, the
bells on their poles
echoing through
the Okunoin.

The view from Saysong Island
VANG VIENG, LAOS.
26 APRIL 2013 1700.
Bicycles and motorbikes rattle across the rickety bridge.
The Song Riv
flows gently pas
it

Getting lost and going beyond in Vang Vieng

Sketching Laos

When my friend Carter and I arrive in Vang Vieng, Laos, for all we know, we could be back in an American college dorm.

This little town has quite the reputation. Set on the Nam Song River, Vang Vieng is a natural hub for outdoor activities such as kayaking and tubing. But combine that with riverside bars offering free shots of Lao-Lao whisky along the way, and you start attracting a different crowd.

And yet the hills surrounding Vang Vieng speak of something different. They lure us away from the town to where the world is just ridges and river – a little more open and a little more pure. We are determined to get lost, to go beyond, to get a closer glimpse of those jagged karst peaks that pierce the sky.

A rickety bridge leads us across the river to long dirt roads that take us nowhere. We walk until Carter mentions we're not getting anywhere fast, and then we turn around and re-trace our steps. Our legs, sore from the sedentary journey from Bangkok, have never been happier.

We follow a network of old bridges to Saysong Island, nothing but a little strip of sea grass and brush between the river's two shorelines. From our perch at a café at the end of the island, life unfolds around us. Children walk their bikes home across the bridge; visiting monks pass in narrow wooden boats, their saffron robes striking against the pale blue water.

In total, we will spend some twenty hours in Vang Vieng – three alone here on Saysong Island, ordering round after round of delectable coconut shakes. And each time I reach the end of another shake, I am reminded that if you're patient and persistent, sometimes there is hidden beauty to be found in a place. You just have to look for it beyond your initial encounter.

You have to look beyond the hills.

Sunday Afternoon Streetscape
LUANG PRABANG, LAOS.
28 APRIL 2013 14.00

Sunday streetscape in Luang Prabang

Sketching Laos

It's a balmy Sunday afternoon in Luang Prabang and before me lies a streetscape my fingers are positively itching to sketch.

On the left, a graceful row of French colonial houses, each with its painted shutters, each with its awnings and balconies forming neat parallel lines.

And on the right side of the street, luscious bunches of bright fuchsia bougainvillea spill across the brick sidewalk, beneath a yellow flowering tree I have yet to find the name for.

It is the exact incarnation of every vision I'd held of Luang Prabang before arriving in this sleepy, UNESCO-preserved town in northern Laos. To finally stand before it – with pen, paints, and sketchbook at the ready – fills me with satisfaction.

The only issue is this: There is nowhere to sketch from.

All the cafés in sight are on the wrong side of the street, tucked away in the very houses I'm wanting to sketch, while the smaller local restaurants on the other side of the street are hidden behind deep folds of flora and foliage.

But then I come across an old wooden table on the sidewalk – a desk, really, with peeling white paint – and a dubiously functional plastic chair, not only set on the side of the street I need, but in a spot affording the precise angle and view I hope to capture. I look around; both table and chair are unoccupied. But not for long.

Out come my sketchbook and paints; within minutes, armed with an iced coffee from a local shop, I am at home at this desk, and the desk feels like home.

Recently, I've been looking at artist-in-residency programs, to give my sketching some kind of official stamp of approval. But today in Luang Prabang, while sketching at a makeshift sidewalk desk, I realize there's only one stamp of approval we need to do what we love.

Our own.

Wat Thoung Sad

LUANG PRABANG, LAOS
29 APRIL 2013 16.00.

Feeling the flow at Wat Thoung Sad Temple

Sketching Laos

With just hours to go before leaving Luang Prabang, I sit down to sketch beneath the awning of a sidewalk café. My subject is a temple, one which a local woman tells me is called Wat Thoung Sad. It has a layered roof, each square section slightly curved and fitted neatly into the next, and a few towering coconut trees beside it.

Almost instantly, I can tell the temple on the page will be what I hope to portray of the temple before me. It's difficult to say how I know this – rather, it's something you can feel: this thing called flow. Every line takes on a life of its own and yet magically connects to every other line. Each curved edge of the roof, each individual vein of a banana leaf, comes out exactly as I'd pictured it – and more so.

Then, in the chatter of tourists behind me, I hear "*arigato gozaimasu*." It has only been five days since I last heard the phrase, and even spoke it myself – one meaning "thank you very much" in Japanese. But here in Laos, which I reached via Bangkok, it feels like it belongs to a different journey altogether.

I turn around and see four Japanese friends ready to leave.

"*Konnichiwa*," I say to them. "I've just been sketching your country!"

They are from various parts of Japan – Kyoto, Chiba, cities in the far north I've never heard of – and I'm delighted to flip back a few pages and share my sketches with them: scenes from Tokyo, Kōyasan, and Shodoshima Island.

As they say goodbye, I reach into my brain and pull back one last phrase from Japan, my favorite: "*Hajime mashite*," which, as the equivalent for "It's nice to meet you," is used when meeting someone for the first time.

To feel the flow of this sketch was more than enough today – but to feel a sense of flow between each part of my journey only increases my gratitude in Luang Prabang.

Patouxay Gate
VIENTIANE, LAOS.
30 APRIL 2013 14.00.
It's warmer here than anywhere else in Laos— but still the breeze is cool.

Unexpected hours and encounters in Vientiane

Sketching Laos

After a long weekend in Luang Prabang, Carter and I descend from the hills into the country's steamy capital of Vientiane.

For days we have been moving around the puzzle pieces of our trip back to Bangkok. When the shifting finally stops and the itinerary of our return has been set, we find ourselves with ten extra hours in Vientiane – and with just one question left to answer: How exactly are we going to fill them?

Naturally, I decide to do a sketch. And because it seems an obvious choice, I choose the iconic Patuxai Gate as my subject – a war monument that was built between 1957 and 1968 in honor of those who fought for independence from the French.

I find a spot on the sidewalk beneath a tree, spread out my scarf, and sit down to sketch, but am immediately feeling the heat, the hard concrete beneath me, and the exhaustion resulting from our all-night journey.

Soon after I start sketching, a boy of about 10 or 11 years cycles past and stops to watch. At first, he stands with one leg on either side of his red-and-green-colored bike, arms resting on the handlebars. A few minutes later, however, I hear a click. He's popped the kickstand out and sits on his haunches next to me, elbows now resting on his knees.

Another half hour goes by before it occurs to me to offer him paper and a pen. Nam and I speak exactly three words of the same language, and yet a sense of connection grows anyhow, as improbable as the tree above us pushing its roots through the sidewalk. We munch on fried sweet potatoes from a nearby cart and sketch with our flip-flops kicked off, passing locals casting bemused glances our way.

It may have taken a while for the ever-shifting puzzle of our day to come together, but here on a Vientiane sidewalk, I'm glad it left room to meet Nam.

angkor wat

SIEM REAP, CAMBODIA.
2 MAY 2013 10.30.

Sharing in the wonder of Angkor Wat

Sketching Cambodia

In the pre-dawn darkness of a still-cool Thursday morning, I hit the streets of Siem Reap, alone on a rusty yellow bike.

Behind my decision to cycle to Angkor Wat was a desire to feel a sense of exploration; to try and channel the sublime sense of discovery French explorer Henri Mouhot must have felt in 1860, when he pushed through dense jungle to find the largest religious monument in the world.

I know all such discoveries have been made by now – but I like to pretend sometimes there's still ground out there to break.

As I near the ticket gate, I revel in being the only bike on the road. Then, two turns before Angkor Wat, I pause by a river to soak up the explosion of dawn, the horizon as vivid as a cracked-open pomegranate, its jewel-like seeds spilling onto the water.

And I soak it up all the more knowing that soon, I will catch up to the crowds already at the temple. So much humanity gathered in one place often overwhelms me, but as I arrive at Angkor Wat in time for sunrise, I'm reminded of an instance when I'm actually okay with it: world wonders.

For some reason, the little part of me that yearns to traverse the globe alone switches off at the sight of such universal icons – and is actually okay with the jutting elbows and the craning of necks and all of us pointing our cameras in the same direction. I'm okay with it because we're somewhere deserving of our wonder, and our very communal presence is a testament to that.

When I return at 10am to sketch the temple, the masses of people have all but dispersed. Once again, I'm alone – but funnily enough, it's the crowds I'm thinking of as I start sketching.

The neck-craning, elbow-jutting crowds – and what it meant to share in the wonder of Angkor Wat aglow at sunrise with them.

Somewhere, incense burns.
occasionally monks pass in dark brown robes.
Noon Night Market
SIEM REAP, CAMBODIA.
3 MAY 2013 22.00

Waiting for inspiration in the Noon Night Market

Sketching Cambodia

I am as unmoved by Siem Reap's Noon Night Market as it gets; impressed only by how scattered and repetitive it seems.

Just about to call it a night, I wander back onto a street that is called, rather understandably, Night Market Road. A neon sign announcing the market hangs at one end, and lights have been strung down the way, giving the market a suddenly festive air. It occurs to me that it's a scene worth sketching if only because it didn't move me at first.

"Let the inspiration come in its own time," I tell myself.

As always, I search for a place to sit – in the best case, a café or restaurant. And here, my only option is the Ababa Curry House.

Some fifteen minutes have gone by when a guy walks up.

"Is the food good?" he asks.

"It's delicious, actually. I can recommend the dal makhani."

He sits down at the table next to me and soon I learn Josh is from Berkeley, was a linguistics major, and that he has been living in Thailand on an agricultural exchange program.

"I'm not a farmer," he says, "but I might be one. One day."

He talks about studying abroad in West Africa and about the poetry workshops he took as a student. Scooping up his own dal makhani with naan bread, he looks over at my sketch. "Wow, you really got the whole scene. I wouldn't know where to start. I only sketch faces and coffee cups, as I usually only sketch in coffeeshops. "

We stay until the street closes, and the rattling of metal gates being brought to the ground echoes from side to side. We walk in opposite directions, back into the Siem Reap night, but the details of Josh's life bounce around in my head for long after we say goodbye, reminding me that we never know who we'll meet, and where.

As always, inspiration had been worth waiting for.

Tuks tuks and
buses kick up
dust.
Below each
house are pick-
up-sticks-like
stilts.
Chong Khneis
Floating Village
SIEM REAP, CAMBODIA.
4 MAY 2013 14.30.

Dry season and disappointment at Chong Khneis

Sketching Cambodia

Ever since arriving in the country, my knowledge of Cambodia has been slowly growing, like rings being added to a tree, year after year.

It began with Siem Reap and Angkor Wat, and has evolved to include Tonlé Sap Lake and the floating villages that exist along its shoreline, forever in flux with the seasons. And before moving on, the village I most want to visit is Kampong Khleang.

Home to some 10,000 people, it is the largest floating village on the lake, and also one of the most remote, its communities of stilted houses difficult to reach from Siem Reap. On the other hand, Chong Khneis is much closer, but I had been warned that with this proximity comes tour buses, and with tour buses come crowds.

As fate would have it, however, I have come to Cambodia in the dry season, when the waters of Tonlé Sap recede. The lake itself shrinks from over 6,000 square miles to just a thousand, and leaves behind a rutted network of roads, nearly impossible to traverse in a tuk tuk. Faced with the facts, I decide to visit Chong Khneis, but I can't help feeling disappointed, like I'm settling for second best.

Within minutes of leaving Siem Reap, the world transitions from city to dusty countryside. Sugarcane fields grow right up to the edge of the road; the air smells of the sea, or more likely of that day's catch brought in and laid out to dry. I spot a lone water buffalo, knee-deep in emerald rice paddies.

"This isn't so bad," I tell myself, content to enjoy the journey, even if the destination isn't what I'd intended.

On the road, as at home, there are things we can't control. And when something as uncontrollable as dry season redirects your path for the day, all you can do is trust that where you are instead is where you're meant to be.

Bracelets and belief at the Killing Fields

Sketching Cambodia

On a gray Sunday afternoon in Phnom Penh, Cambodia, I arrive at the Choeung Ek Genocidal Center – a site better known as the Killing Fields.

And almost as soon as I begin to wander its oddly tranquil paths, past the Memorial Stupa housing 5,000 human skulls from those killed by the Khmer Rouge, I can see that I was meant to come here; that I was meant to see the bracelets.

I see three mass graves during my time at Choeung Ek – one is home to 450 victims, while another is filled with the bodies of Khmer Rouge soldiers, those whom Pol Pot accused of having a "Cambodian body, but Vietnamese head."

Today the graves are protected beneath open-air shelters and surrounded by bamboo fences – and on each and every fence post there are bracelets: brightly colored friendship bracelets, ones made from ribbons, and others that read *Cambodia* on their sides. Thousands and thousands of bracelets – and for whatever reason, they are what move me the most.

I slip a bracelet off my wrist, an orange one I found on a street in Laos. I'd read they are an important part of Baci ceremonies, tied around a person's wrist for good luck, and so I had worn it ever since to remind me of my time there. Now I leave it here, above a bracelet the color of blood.

And, so it seems, have so many others, slipping off whatever they had on their wrist at the time and leaving it behind – as an act of love, or belief, or perhaps of prayer. Because what else can you do at a place where a million people died – and at the hand of their own countrymen?

What else can you do but think and hope and pray and believe for healing and leave something, anything, behind that says we were here, and that we remember?

The Killing Fields

CHOEUNG EK, PHNOM PENH, CAMBODIA.
5 MAY 2013 16.30.

Dominoes and decisions in a Saigon beer garden

Sketching Vietnam

I'm on my way to the Ben Thanh Night Market when I see them: my beloved red lanterns, three even rows of them, strung across the courtyard of the Bier Garden.

It isn't something I would stop to sketch normally – a restaurant, and a pricy, foreigner-dominated restaurant at that, with dance music (a la Rihanna, Katy Perry, and Usher) pulsing overhead.

But these red paper lanterns, so beautifully aglow, have come to yield a strong pull on me, and almost against my will I'm sitting down at a table, ordering a draft Tiger beer, and getting to work.

The gold tassels hanging from each lantern sway in the listless breeze. The expats behind me discuss the relative merits of living in Singapore vs. Sydney vs. Saigon, while outside the gate a shoe shiner stops to work, pulling out tools from the little wooden box they each carry. He takes one tennis shoe and then the other, scrubbing each to a gleaming white perfection, and then he leaves, box once again hung from the crook of his elbow.

And what's going through my mind is this: I wasn't supposed to be here. Not only was I meant to be in India until now, but even once this sketching trip initially came together, Vietnam was nowhere on the itinerary.

But thanks to a question from an editor – *are you going to Ho Chi Minh City soon?* – I am here, each decision having led to the next like a series of dominoes, as surely as one lantern leads to another on the rows now swaying above my head.

So that's what I'm feeling for the thousandth time on this journey – gratitude for the world, for each culture that forms a part of it, and for the chance to dip my toes in each new way of life.

While I keep waiting for an encounter or an epiphany to occur, tonight it is enough to sketch alone beneath the glow of seventeen red lanterns.

I sketch to the beat of dance music and remixes.
Bier Garden Saigon
HO CHI MINH CITY, VIETNAM.
7 MAY 2013 19.00.
shiner
ist outside
the gate.

French and Spanish swirl in the air.
Central Post Office
SAIGON, VIETNAM.
8 MAY 2013 15.00.

Serendipity in the Saigon Central Post Office

Sketching Vietnam

She appears in a blur of purple and pink, motioning for me to move my bags aside so that she can have a seat on the bench.

It's hard to blame her – the Saigon Central Post Office is packed on this Wednesday afternoon. I have a feeling that with its century of history and regal arched ceiling, it's a tourist attraction in all types of weather, but clearly even more so today, as visitors flock inside after rainclouds let loose over the city.

After all, that's what drove me to draw here – as a way of staying on top of my sketches while also escaping the showers. And at first, it is seriously slow going. I survey my sketch after an hour: Apart from a quick outline in pencil, I've managed to do exactly one section of the ceiling in pen. Only thirteen more to go.

But then she arrives, a girl around my age in a long skirt and scarf the same shade of dark pink. She sits down, pulls a book out of her backpack, and extends it towards me, her arms straight out and a huge smile on her face. I have no idea what's going on.

I take the book from her and crack it open with great hesitance. The fact that she has yet to say a word only adds to my bewilderment. What greets me first is a colorful drawing of rice paddies; on the next page, a Cambodian farmer in a conical straw hat with his cow. And then I get it: She's a fellow sketch artist.

Her name is Ksyucha, she's from St. Petersburg, Russia, and she has spent the last seven months working in Thailand as a guide for Russian tourists. We talk briefly about our travels but are soon swapping sketchbooks, looking through each other's drawings, and even comparing what mediums we use (she prefers colored pencils and markers; I prefer watercolors).

It is such serendipities that I have come to live for – no matter how long the sketch itself may take to complete.

Friends and forgiveness at Reunification Palace

Sketching Vietnam

On my last morning in Saigon, there is one place I have left to sketch: the Reunification Palace.

Built in 1966, it played a central role in the Vietnam War, serving as the headquarters of South Vietnam's president, and later, as the setting for the Fall of Saigon, after a North Vietnamese tank barreled through its gates. I'd passed it the previous night with two new friends, college students named Hà and Nhan.

"You know this place? It is Independence Palace," Nhan said, referring to the building by its former name. "You know war? Between Vietnam and America?"

I said I did, and on the tip of my tongue, perched as lightly as a diver on the edge of a platform, were two words: *I'm sorry*.

I had felt this way before, in the Foreigners' Registration Office in Delhi. While I stood in line to receive a number to wait in yet another line, I spoke with the girl next to me, her dark hair covered by a red headcloth.

"Where are you from?" she asked, after telling me her name was Zhila. I had seen her passport and answered with hesitance. Zhila was from Iran.

"Ah, American," she said. "Iran and USA are, you know..."

"I know." Once again I felt the need to apologize or explain myself. "But it is nice to meet *you*." I didn't want something as out of our control as our nationalities to get in the way.

And so as I spend my last hours in Saigon sketching the palace, I break down reunification, strip away the prefix and the suffix, and get to the heart of the word, "unify": to make or become united. Because isn't that what travel – and more specifically, connection – is about?

Accepting the differences we can't change and acknowledging that what unites us everywhere is the same thing that united me with Hà and Nhan and Zhila:

A simple little thing called friendship.

Independence Palace
SAIGON, VIETNAM.
10 MAY 2013 13.00
At 1pm sharp, the fountain is switched on.
e signature melody
the ice cream sellers
reaches me even here.

Connections and bridges over a Bangkok canal

Sketching Thailand

They find me nearly as soon as I start sketching above Bangkok's Sansab Canal – two bright-eyed local children, possibly the cutest kids I could ever hope to meet in this city of nine million people.

Their names are Masalee and Asamawee, and it isn't long before we're all drawing on the bridge together, our pages filling up with scenes of life along the water. For a moment, I forget about my own sketch as I marvel at how deftly they wield first a pen, and then a paintbrush.

If I didn't believe it after meeting Nam in Laos, I believe it now: Art is innate in all of us.

It's my last weekend in the city, and my last weekend before this sketching trip comes to its inevitable end, but this isn't my first time at the canal. Some three and a half years earlier, I'd visited it on my first trip to Thailand, the same boats plying the narrow channel of water while the same ice cream sellers passed on the sidewalk below, their bells jingling in the air.

Upon returning to the canal today, this time to sketch it, I had expected to feel a sense of connection with this place, having stood here once before. But the connection that moves me the most this Saturday afternoon isn't with the place itself, but with these two kids I've been fortunate enough to meet – who leave their sketch on a chair at the bottom of the bridge.

Because that's what this trip has been as well: a bridge between home and away, a passage that is both beginning and end.

I take their painting with me when I leave some time after them – as a reminder of our serendipitous sketching session, and as a token of my gratitude that something as simple as a sketch could open the door to our encounter.

Here in Southeast Asia, as on every journey, it is the people who have made each place.

Sansab Canal
BANGKOK, THAILAND.
11 MAY 2013 17.00

Sketching Serendipities

The incredible encounters that unfolded as I sketched in each place are moments I now treasure as much as the sketches themselves. Here are some of the fellow sketch artists I am grateful to have met.

Tan – Chong Khneis, Cambodia

Hà Mã – Ho Chi Minh City, Vietnam

Nam – Vientiane, Laos

Quang Tiep & Mai –
Ho Chi Minh City

Ksyucha –
Ho Chi Minh City

Masalee & Asamawee –
Bangkok, Thailand

Travel Resources

A few suggestions of where to eat, stay, and play to kick off your own adventures in Southeast Asia and Japan.

Singapore

➳ **EAT: Istanbul Grill and Café**
Succulent lamb kebabs, paprika-dusted hummus, and a killer mint tzatziki sauce are just a few reasons to dine *al fresco* here in the shadow of the Sultan Mosque. 62 Bussorah Street. (+65) 6296 4084.

➳ **BIKE: Cycling down East Coast Park**
Head to East Coast Park for a perfect Sunday afternoon in the city, tracing the coast of the Singapore Strait on two wheels (or really test your balance on a tandem). 1013 East Coast Parkway. (+65) 6445 1147.

➳ **DRINK: Bar Stories**
This one-of-a-kind cocktail bar is tucked away in the Arab Street neighborhood; tell the bartenders what kind of mood you're in and they'll create a custom drink for you. 55/57A Haji Lane. www.barstories.com.sg

Malaysia

➳ **GET THERE: Day train from Singapore**
Only seven hours away by train, overland is the way to go to Kuala Lumpur. It's cheaper to pre-book tickets from Johor Bahru (JB) to KL on www.ktmb.com.my, and then buy a ticket to JB at Woodlands Station.

➳ **GO: Exploring to Pulau Ketam**
Home to several Chinese fishing villages, this peaceful island is a short trip from Kuala Lumpur; take the KMUTER train to Port Klang (1.5 hours, $1.40), and then it's a 45-minute local ferry ride to the island.

➳ **STAY: Sea Lion Inn**
There are few frills at Pulau Ketam's largest hotel, but it is conveniently located right at the end of the main ferry jetty; single rooms start at $9 per night. (+60) 3-3110 4121. www.sealion.com.my

Laos

➳ GET THERE: Night train from Bangkok
Although it has a tendency to run late, the night train is still an excellent way to reach Laos; book tickets at the main Hualamphong Railway Station in Bangkok. Tickets for 2nd class sleeper with A/C start at $23.

➳ GO: Kayaking in Vang Vieng
This backpacker hotspot may have a certain reputation, but beyond its main streets lie beautifully open fields, karst hills, and the quiet Nam Song River all waiting to be explored. www.greendiscoverylaos.com

➳ STAY: La Résidence Phou Vao, Luang Prabang
Set just outside the heart of Luang Prabang, this Orient Express hotel feels like an elegant mountain retreat, with exquisite views of the hills and valleys below. (+856) 72 212194. www.residencephouvao.com

Cambodia

➳ STAY: La Résidence d'Angkor, Siem Reap
Treat yourself to a bit of laid-back luxury at this Orient Express property; at the very least, be sure to stop by for happy hour cocktails in the Martini Lounge. (+855) 63 963 390. www.residencedangkor.com

➳ BIKE: Cycling to Angkor Wat
Although you can hire a tuk tuk to visit the temples, it's also fun to get there by your own momentum. Bike rentals in Siem Reap start at the wonderfully affordable rate of $1 per day. www.angkor-cycling-tour.com

➳ VISIT: Choeung Ek Genocidal Center, Phnom Penh
Better known as the Killing Fields, this site is a memorial to the thousands of Cambodians murdered here in the 1970s. Admission is $3 for foreign visitors and includes a well-narrated, enlightening audio guide.

Vietnam

➼ **STAY: My My Art House Hotel, Ho Chi Minh City**
A few artistic touches make this basic guesthouse stand out; standard single private room with private bath starts at $12.50 per night. 219/8 Pham Ngu Lao Street. (+84) 8-3836 7937. arthousehotel@yahoo.com

➼ **EAT: Pho Nho, HCMC**
Not only is the *pho* here prepared Hanoi-style (and thus delicious), but the walls are covered in charming murals depicting street scenes from the northern city. 170 Nguyen Dinh Chieu. (+84) 8-3930 5739.

➼ **DRINK: Vung oi mo ra Café (or Café Vung), HCMC**
This is the kind of place you would hardly know is there from the street; chill out with an iced coffee, soak up the great atmosphere, and catch live music every night. 17 Ngô Thoi Nhiem. (+84) 8-2215 7813.

Thailand

➼ **SAIL: Chao Phraya Tourist Boat, Bangkok**
Leave Bangkok's bustling streets behind for life on the river, getting to sights such as the Grand Palace, Wat Pho, and Wat Arun by boat; a one-day river pass is 150 Baht ($5). www.chaophrayaexpressboat.com

➼ **EAT & DRINK: Asiatique the Riverfront**
Open from 5pm-midnight, head to this new complex for happy hour and al fresco dining on the river – not to mention some night market-style shopping. 2194 Charoenkrung 72-74 Road. www.thaiasiatique.com

➼ **GO: Tha Kha Floating Market**
This market in Samut Songkhram is one of the least touristic floating markets around Bangkok and makes for a perfect daytrip from the city; catch a bus to Samut Songkhram from the Southern Bus Terminal.

Japan

➼ **HIKE: 88-Temple Circuit, Shodoshima Island**
This trail is a shorter version of the Buddhist pilgrimage of the same name on Shikoku Island; at just 100 miles long (160 kilometers), the Shodoshima circuit takes less time (7-8 days) but is just as rewarding.

➼ **LEARN: En Tea Ceremony Experience, Kyoto**
This beautiful one-hour tea ceremony takes you behind the scenes of a centuries-old tradition; the experience is 2,000 Yen per person ($20) and in English. (+81) 080-3782-2706. www.teaceremonyen.com

➼ **STAY: Kōyasan Guest House Kokuu, Kōyasan**
You traditionally stay in a temple in this holy city, but a stylish new hostel provides an affordable alternative; cozy mountain capsules start at $35 a night. (+81) 0736-26-7216. www.koyasanguesthouse.com

About the Author

Candace Rose Rardon is a writer, photographer, and sketch artist originally from the state of Virginia, although she has also called the UK, New Zealand, and India home. She graduated Phi Beta Kappa from the University of Virginia, and in 2012, received her Masters in Travel Writing from London's Kingston University. Since her first sketching trip to Porto, Portugal, two and a half years ago, Candace has sketched her way through 15 countries and now can't imagine ever traveling without her sketchbook. Visit her website, *The Great Affair,* at www.candaceroserardon.com.

44106075R00033

Made in the USA
Lexington, KY
22 August 2015